The Silver Brigade

A read-aloud story for children

MARILEE MARDELL

Introduction

The first time I saw the home of the little silver-clad soldiers was somewhere over the Great Lakes on a flight from Toronto to Winnipeg.

Almost every trip over the lakes is a bumpy one. Just as you raise your cup of hot coffee to your lips, you suddenly find it hitting your nose instead. Your fork dips down for some mashed potatoes and never reaches them; your tray has suddenly dropped out of range – very disconcerting.

I generally try to get my mind off the unpredictable drops by gazing out of the window. On one memorable flight my gaze was particularly pleasantly rewarded. Huge thunderclouds were piled up to an enormous height below our jetliner. The rays of the setting sun lit up the mile-high smooth white mounds.

Suddenly my attention was caught by something strange picked out by the last rays. Yes, those were distinctly caves tucked into the mountainous clouds, and higher up what appeared to be a castle surrounded by rolling white hills. Faintly, I seemed to hear tinkly laughter as ...

Well, why don't you sit down, get comfortable and hear all about it.

Chapter 1

Raam rolled over on his side with a low growl. He was finding it quite difficult to get the troops together. Soon Barak would be flinging down the bright pathway and his troops were supposed to be in marching order. What were they up to now, the little rascals?

In a moment Raam spied Seren, captain of the Twinklies, hurrying past with a pearly ball in his hand.

"Now where are you going so fast?" growled Raam. "You know that the troops are supposed to be ready. Bora's orders, of course."

"I know, I know," Seren answered quickly. He seemed in a dreadful hurry. "But can't you just let us finish our game of bowls? Our team was winning when our best ball slipped through a crack. Of course it must have fallen all the way down…" His voice faded out; dropping a ball could spell trouble.

"That was careless, to say the least," frowned Raam. "We have no orders to send down hailstones. Dancing diamonds! Why must you fellows make life so difficult for me?" And with another great rumble, Raam turned over to his other side. Seren took the chance to speed away while his back was turned.

Why was their fun always spoiled with a work order? Even Seren, chief of the Silver Brigade, loved play more than work. Besides, these missions were highly dangerous at times. And sometimes your best friends did not return to Cloudland and its safe caves.

7

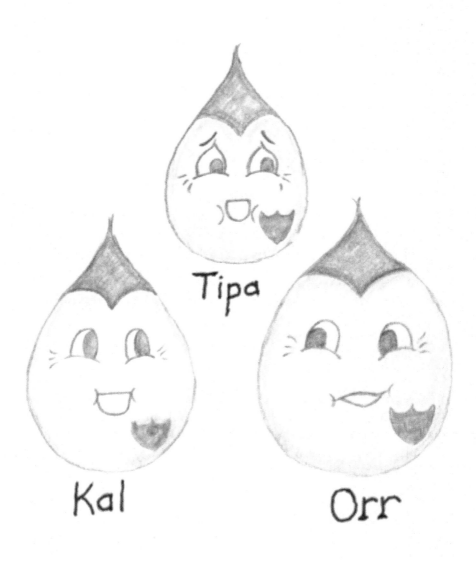

Seren now rolled more slowly, thoughtfully, into the cave where tinkly laughter bounced from wall to wall. Scores of little Twinklies were throwing shiny white balls down lanes of ice, trying to knock down the icicles set up at the far end.

"Time to move, fellas!" called Seren above the echoing voices. "Raam is in a growly mood. You know what that means. He'll probably send us down super-fast. Come on!"

The three Twinklies nick-named "Trio" looked at each other anxiously. It was to be their very first mission and there was no hiding it – they were scared! What if they got separated down below? Or even worse… but no, they would not let such terrible thoughts even stay in their heads.

The Trio was the last to form ranks on the rolling fields where Raam was growling out orders. Row upon row of tiny troops dressed in shiny silver lined up in marching order.

They did not think of themselves as odd because they had no feet. No one in Cloudland had any. Certainly not Raam or Barak. Bora might have – but no one ever saw Bora. He was the Commander-in-chief. You would not want to disobey him any less than going uninvited to the high castle where he lived.

The Trio, three inseparable pals, were Orr, Kal and Tipa. Up till now they had rolled up and down the round white hills of Cloudland happily playing games, or singing in the great Twinklies Glee Club in the huge rainbow-colored dome where many events were held. And sometimes they enjoyed a sherbet in the canteen.

There was not much difference in the looks of any of the Twinklies; it was their insignias, their size and their eyes by which one could tell them apart. The Trio all belonged to the same brigade, whose insignia was a purple patch on the front of the silver uniform.

Orr, who was a bit bigger and older than his pals, also had a tiny zigzag motif on his patch to show that he would some day work closely with Barak.

9

Kal had a tiny black circle at the top of the purple patch to show that Storm Chief would sometimes be his commander. Kal won all the races in Cloudland, it seemed to his friends. Already he had a reputation of speed in a brigade of fast-moving soldiers.

Little Tipa, the smallest of Twinklies, had no special marking as yet. Some day he hoped to do something really brave. But right now he was not feeling brave at all.

"Do you have your secret equipment?" whispered Orr.

"Roger!" Kal nodded. But Tipa pulled his out from under his tunic, just to make sure.

No Twinkly should leave Cloudland without the special device Bora had designed for their return to Cloudland after a mission, or for their rescue in time of need. It was a tiny solar reflector; tiny, but powerful enough to be monitored thousands of feet above the Bottomlands, as earth was called.

"Let's stick together on the way down," Kal whispered.

"Oh, for sure!" replied Tipa. "Whatever would I do without you guys?" The thought made him shiver with fright. But Raam was barking out final orders and everyone was at attention. There was no more time to put secret fears into words.

"There's a fire burning out of control below us. In a few minutes we'll be directly overhead. As soon as Barak lets down the pathway, ROLL! All of you!" And he seemed to look sternly at little Tipa. "Keep together and do your best. This afternoon we'll beam you up."

Chapter 2

Listening in on Raam's instructions had been a playful little breeze. Of course, the winds had to be in on the plan of action for they had an important part to play in directing the Silver Brigade's movements. But they worked under strict orders of Bora, just like everyone else.

Naughty little Gusty, however, had not yet learned that disobeying Bora's orders could have serious consequences. He would find that out. An idea began to hatch in his airy little brain. He could have some fun with the little guys. Just let old Mizra, chief of the East Winds, turn his stern attention somewhere else while he played his tricks.

*** *** ***

Many miles north and east of Winnipeg firefighters wiped the soot and sweat from their faces as they caught their breath. This forest fire was hard to get under control. Some of the men were near exhaustion. If help didn't come soon, they would have to give up and let the fire burn itself out unchecked.

The sky was totally shut out by thick clouds of smoke. If the sun was shining, the firefighters wouldn't know it. Neither could they see the heavy black clouds moving in from the east.

Grimly the men continued to beat the burning ground fire, hoping all the while that as the crown fire leaped from tree to tree above them that they would not be trapped in the inferno. That and exhaustion were their greatest dangers, besides breathing in the smoke.

Meanwhile, up in Cloudland the troops were ready and waiting. Mizra and his crew had brought the Silver Brigade directly over the flaming forest. But the firefighters still didn't know it.

A brilliant flash and a long crooked fork of light flamed through the dark sky. Instantly Raam boomed out his order in a roar that could be heard for miles. The Silver Brigade was on its way!

Down the path of light rushed thousands of tiny troops dressed in their silver uniforms, coming to the aid of the tired firefighters. As they descended in a great rush on flash after flash by Barak, Raam roared and growled orders and encouragement.

"Stick with me, guys!" yelled Orr to his friends as the Trio leapt onto the shining path.

"Roger!" panted Kal. But there was no response from Tipa.

As they rushed down, down towards the Bottomlands, Orr could feel the heat from the forest fire. He hoped they would survive. Just before they hit bottom, Orr heard one of the fire-fighters give a sigh of relief. "Thank God!" he breathed. "We'll make it now."

Orr landed safely as did Kal. Together with hundreds of other Twinklies they managed to put out the flames. The shock troops, the first Twinklies to descend, had vanished as the fierce flames swallowed them up in sizzles and steam. These were the older Twinklies who had been on many and varied missions. Were they lost forever? Orr and Kal didn't know.

Soon only smoke hissed from the still hot ground. The Twinklies felt uncomfortably warm. If only they could hold their shape till the afternoon!

Chapter 3

The naughty little breeze, Gusty, meanwhile, had played his mean trick. Just as the little silver soldiers were sliding to the Bottomlands, he gave a great puff in the wrong direction. Oddly enough, he only managed to divert one little Twinkly, and that was poor Tipa.

"Hey!" he yelled in panic. "Quit that! You're blowing me off course!" But it was too late. Tipa flew slantwise to the south and finally landed in a garden. He didn't know it was a garden. After all, this was his first mission, his first descent to the Bottomlands. And now he was separated from Orr and Kal. He was terrified.

"Pssst! Over here!" whispered a tinkly voice that sounded strangely like Kal's. Tipa peered eagerly in the direction from which the whisper came. It was not his friend Kal, but someone who looked very much like him except for the insignia.

"Who are you?" whispered Tipa, without knowing why they were whispering.

"I saw you land all by yourself," answered the stranger. "How come you're all alone? Usually the Twinklies come in companies."

"I was blown off course by a nasty little breeze. But who <u>are</u> you? You sound just like my friend, Kal. He's one of the swiftest Twinklies," he couldn't help boasting a bit.

"I'm Tal," replied the other. "I stay in the Bottomlands most of the time. That is, my missions are always here, but I have been up in Cloudland once. I was so frightened when I came rushing down the bright shiny path. I thought there would be nothing left of me."

"I thought it was kind of fun," declared Tipa, not too truthfully and trying to sound brave. "Where are we and how do I get back to the Silver Brigade?" he asked.

"Shhh! Not so loud! There are awful creatures always on the lookout for a Twinkly. You don't want to get swallowed, do you?"

Horrified, Tipa looked anxiously around. Everything was so strange in this new world of the Bottomlands. He could see Tal now.

He was resting on something broad and green. Tipa had landed on a hard gray surface. All around were tall green things, but Tipa could also see a huge round bowl on a tall stem. He had no idea what these things were.

Tal's eyes opened wide in fear as he hissed: "Don't move! There's that thing people call a robin hopping over this way!"

Poor Tipa! What was a 'robin' and what was 'people' anyway? He lay as still as he could while trembling with fear. Too bad Orr and Kal weren't here; they would know what to do. All he could think of was his pals; he had completely forgotten his secret solar instrument with which he could signal Bora for help

"I have a plan," whispered Tal softly. "I'll attract the monster's attention and you roll underneath this leaf I'm on so it can't see you."

"Oh, but... but that will be dang- "

"Just do it!" hissed Tal. At the same time he rolled a little further down the leaf. Sure enough, the robin turned its bright black eye toward him. Meanwhile, Tipa carefully pulled back under the shade of the green thing Tal had called a leaf.

Now Tal was not as brave, or as crazy, as Tipa might think. He knew, although Tipa did not, that his time of sitting outside was almost up. At any moment now he would slip back into the green leaf until after dark. But would that happen soon enough to keep him from being swallowed by the robin?

Chapter 4

All this time Orr and Kal were wondering what had happened to their pal, Tipa. They were really worried about the little Twinkly, but how could they do anything before they got back to Cloudland?

They had some worries of their own, too. If the sun didn't come out, they might sink down into the ground and then not even their secret solar devices would help them get back to Cloudland. Not for days, maybe years.

A soft breeze sent by Darom, the South Wind, swept over the large group of Twinklies huddled together with Orr and Kal. His whisper brought a tinkly cheer from all of them. "The sun is coming out," were his encouraging words.

Every Twinkly immediately pulled out his solar device and aimed it at the sun. Raam's promise was going to be kept this time. Sure enough, after a time the little soldiers in their silver uniforms slipped upward, one after the other, in an invisible stream, sliding up the beam of light the sun sent down for them.

Thankfully they all gathered to report to Seren, their captain.

"Form ranks!" commanded Seren in his silvery voice. No matter how hard he tried to bark and growl like Raam, his orders always came out sounding like music. But the Twinklies obeyed.

"Roll call!" was the next command. One after the other the little soldiers called out their names. It sounded like silver chimes. Sadly Orr and Kal called out their names, missing little Tipa.

Seren noticed the omission of Tipa, the only one of this unit missing. "What happened to Tipa?" he demanded of the other two members of the Trio.

"We have no idea," answered Orr, with downcast eyes. "He was right behind us when we got on the shiny pathway, wasn't he Kal?"

"Roger! But he didn't answer when Orr asked if we were all together. Then we slid down so fast we couldn't stop and look for him."

"Of course, of course," Seren replied hurriedly. "Okay, we'll see what information Mizra's couriers might have. I know you guys miss him. I'll do my best. Dismissed!" Then the troops were free to retire to the caves of Cloudland for a well-earned rest.

Gusty was trying to hide when Seren approached Mizra to ask about Tipa. It didn't take a minute, though, for Mizra to call him in a voice that left him no choice but to come forward. He remembered, a little too late, that Bora could see everything and everybody, all the time. There was no hiding from him, and he, of course, would have let Mizra know what his bad little breeze had done.

"Own up, Gusty! Where did you send Tipa?" demanded Mizra in his stern voice.

"I...I was just having fun," pouted the breeze.

"Disobeying orders is not fun! It is trouble for someone else. And now it means trouble for you too."

"Where did you send him?" asked Seren, concerned for his smallest silver soldier.

"I...think...south," stammered Gusty.

"I will send down a rescue squad, if Raam agrees," Seren decided, "and you will lead the way." He frowned at the breeze.

Mizra added, "Bora has already decided your punishment, too. You will be tied up in the East Wind Cave long enough for you to learn your lesson."

"Oh no!" cried Gusty. "I can't stand that!"

"You will stand it and you will learn!" declared Mizra in a 'no nonsense' voice. "Get your rescue team ready, Seren."

Chapter 5

Tipa shivered and rolled farther back out of sight. "Tal," he whispered. No answer. Peeping out, Tipa saw the robin monster hopping away. But Tal was nowhere in sight.

Suddenly Tipa heard a wonderful sound, the swish of Twinklies rushing past. "Hurray!" he yelled, though his yell was only a tinkle.

It was only a small rescue team and Mizra sent them down, not Barak and Raam. In the lead was Gusty. He was as surprised as Seren that he had found the garden. But nobody could see Tipa as they settled wherever they landed.

"Orr, where are we?" asked Kal, looking around.

"No idea. I don't see Tipa, that's for sure. We seem to be in a round bowl." Orr was right. They had landed in a birdbath, with no way of getting near Tipa. Seren and a few other Twinklies had also splashed in with them.

"Now what, Seren?" asked Orr.

"Wait. That's all we can do for now." Seren was not too happy at their odd landing place. He couldn't see anything but Cloudland high above them. If Bora didn't help them out somehow, Tipa wouldn't be found and rescued.

Just at that moment a shadow loomed above them. The robin monster had hopped onto the edge of the birdbath. Before the Twinklies had time to wink or think, it plopped down right in their midst and started shaking them up. They didn't know he was having a bath. All they knew was that suddenly they were flying through the air without the help of Mizra.

Orr and Kal landed softly, together with Seren and the others, on the hard gray surface Tipa had been sitting on when he first landed. Tipa had a shock when he saw them and called out eagerly: "Over here!"

"Hey! Where are you, Tipa?" asked Seren. "Show yourself."

Tipa rolled out from under the leaf, looking around for the robin monster at the same time. "Over here!"

"Way to go! You're safe!" yelled Orr and Kal in unison.

"Solar reflectors, everyone!" snapped Seren. "Let's get back to Cloudland. Look! There comes the sun!"

Sure enough, late afternoon sunbeams were just reaching down into the garden. But the robin had finished its bath and was down on the ground, hopping all about. There was no time to lose.

Every Twinkly had his secret instrument ready. Before the robin could even see them twinkle, up they slipped, back to Cloudland. Safe!

Gusty got back to Cloudland, too, but he was blown up by Mizra, who wouldn't let him out of his sight until he was safely tied up in the Cave of the East Wind. Did he learn his lesson?

The Trio rolled happily over the hills of Cloudland.

"Let's go have a sherbet in the Canteen," suggested Orr.

"Roger!" agreed Kal.

But Tipa said nothing. He was quietly thanking Bora for bringing him safely back to Cloudland. "And I'll try never again to forget my secret device," he whispered.

As for Gusty, after several boring and lonely weeks in the Cave of the East wind, he humbly begged to be set free. For a long time, at least in his opinion, he behaved himself. Of course, new adventures would follow all of them in days to come.

*** *** ***

CPSIA information can be obtained
at www.ICGtesting.com
Printed in the USA
LVOW01s0847020216
473237LV00005B/7/P